For Julie,
Love, Virginia
12/2007

Illuminated Heart

Love Songs of a Zen Romantic

To Julie
with lots of
Fig Love

Illuminated Heart

Love Songs of a Zen Romantic

Pastels Julie Higgins

Poems Joe Pulichino

RAVZEN PRESS

SAN FRANCISCO, CALIFORNIA

Ravzen Press

773 Chestnut Street

San Francisco, CA 94133

www.zenromantic.com

PRINTED IN CHINA

FIRST EDITION

ISBN: 978-0-9797775-3-0

LIBRARY OF CONGRESS CONTROL NUMBER: 2007932144

"Despite all the troubles in the world, in my heart
I have never given up on the love in which I was brought up
or on man's hope in love. In life, just as on the artist's palette,
there is but one single color that gives meaning
to life and art… the color of love."

MARC CHAGALL

We dedicate this book to Love
and all the lovers
who remain faithfully romantic and inspired by Love
whether they have experienced
one love or many.

TABLE OF CONTENTS

Note: appearance of one of the section symbols (   ) at the bottom of a poem page indicates the continuation of a poem stanza onto the following page.

PREFACE

This is a book full to the spilling-over with love—not ideas about the thing but the thing itself—evoked and expressed in words and images that are sensual, tender, and witty all at the same time. Take this poetic moment from "A Moment with the Kittatiny" (page 19):

> granite, ice coming, and the wind sheets
> of this fruit shaking autumn day
>
> tell me:
> there are no dead things in this world.
>
> rocks trickle down mountainsides and leaves
> spiral to remind us of the pause
>
> incessant in the rhythm of things;
> circles of wind dry the sweat from the palm
>
> of my hand outstretched as I turn to you
> running down Appalachian corridors
>
> of this one world, this one time.

There are no dead things in the world of this book—love makes everything come alive, as much in the fruit shaking autumn as in the lushness of summer, alive and bursting out with its exuberance and fecundity. Take the pastel that accompanies "To My Young Fig" (page 35). Here is a summer fruitfulness in every sense complementing the autumnal Kittatiny and offering its own response to the hand outstretched. The fig is as full of fruit and seed as the woman whose entrance to her fruit and seed the fig resembles. She is confidently and comfortably aware of this natural analogy and does not find it at all salacious, nor does the amused raven, who smiles proudly at the discovery of these resemblances. The curves of the hills and fields resemble the curves of the fruit-full woman and like her are governed in their cycles by the same celestial forces marked throughout the book by sunshine, moon slivers, and shooting stars. A rich world of the senses waiting to become even richer when man and woman meet, as they do on page after page in words and images.

You won't get tired of turning the pages of this book over and over again, because the person who is tired of love is tired of life.

— William Vesterman, PhD, ASSOCIATE PROFESSOR OF ENGLISH, RUTGERS UNIVERSITY

O, the stories these pastels and poems tell—the exhilarating highs of love, the painful lows, the passions and confusions! Stories filled with sensual abundance, deep reflection, and most delightfully—an earthy, robust sexuality. As the book opens, we hear the first notes of love's melody—faint, sweet, enticing, becoming more clear as the heart awakens. Then we dance to the rhythms of love—the joys and sorrows that come as lovers play and work to blend two beats. Finally, we celebrate the harmonies of love and that sweet happily ever after that eventually comes to all of us. Together, these beautiful pastels and poems tell one story really—that big lifetime love story we all know so well. Go pick some fresh fruit, pour a glass of wine, enjoy!

—Athena Vittorio, PSYCHOLOGIST AND AUTHOR, ROME, ITALY

Sensitivity and passion illuminate the words and images of this lovely book. Chronicling the depth of feeling in a look, a touch, a kiss, the longing of an unconceived child to be born…softness and quiet become a meditation.

—Bill Kane, ARTIST, PETALUMA, CALIFORNIA

...and you see the perfect manicure

and glistening dew of the lawn

and hear the soft distant tap

of the raven's beak on hardwood...

melody...

Too Late Too Soon

sometimes,
what appears to be too late,
turns out to be too soon;

you think the party has peaked
and turning back into the night
you leave before the one guest
you longed for first arrives.

and she, coming through the door,
not finding you,
wonders where you've gone
and whether you've slipped away
simply because you've confused
the light of dawn
for the light of dusk;

the guest neither waits
nor disappears
and in one moment coming
you do meet her, neither too late
nor too soon,
and you see the perfect manicure
and glistening dew of the lawn,
and hear the soft distant tap
of the raven's beak
on hardwood.

Elk Island

I.

we paddle there in canoes
pull ourselves around its curves
follow inlets and meadows
where mountain storms
have whistled down the trees
we circle Elk Island once
before sunlight trembles into dusk

II.

on Elk Island we find moose bones
and ponds of black water
make bone drums
to beat before the driftwood fires
throbbing night sound over wave

III.

we make no garlands with the columbine
scattered as they are upon the hillside
we run past them
breathing them all
stepping on some
leaving them bending
to the shadow of mountain

IV.

the wind blows down the canyon
over waves in Jackson Lake
clouds cover Mount Moran
rain drifts
we sit in the flapping blue tent
playing cards
waiting

16

V.

on Elk Island we grow
three day beards and dream
of bursting into crowded bar rooms
looking for women
and chanting the names of stars

VI.

when women sleep here
we watch them, hidden
from a ledge we see them leaving
in the wake of morning
putting tents in canoes
the sound of their paddles
reach us

VII.

they slip away
out of sight
past other islands
on the lake
floating with pine

A Moment with the Kittatiny

Living rocks and leaves do not crumble
on this trail beneath our footsteps

lightly they shock the soles
with sound and hard edges;

granite, ice coming, and the wind sheets
of this fruit shaking autumn day

tell me:
there are no dead things in this world.

Rocks trickle down mountainsides and leaves
spiral to remind us of the pause

incessant in the rhythm of things;
circles of wind dry the sweat from the palm

of my hand outstretched as I turn to you
running down Appalachian corridors

of this one world, this one time.

Slowness of Mountain,

I.

fresh hearts flowering,
new vulnerabilities,
softness of water

20

II.

breathing sitting still
leaving you, alone right now;
slowness of mountain

III.

softness of water
soothing change; melting glaciers
slowness of mountain

Softness of Water

When You Are Ready

when you are ready
you will know
surely as earth knowing
precisely that time
when her own soil
completes the slow unfreezing,
and warming
under that patient protective sky,
she asks for the rains of spring,
she, ready for blossom.

in your moment of knowing
you will be ready,
surely pulling the dreaming sky
with its panoply of stars and whispers
to your valleys and seas
your crests and canyons,
and warming
in that settling of earth and sky,
you ask for the lightening of heaven,
you, ready for blossom.

...letting love in, letting love out.

keeping the self whole,

dancing to its rhythms,

its singular discrete code...

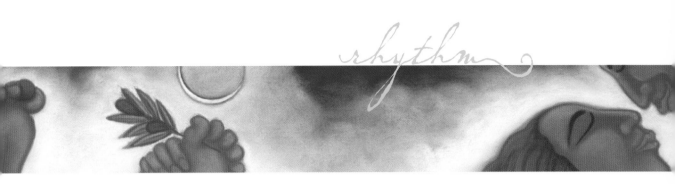

rhythm

at the museum last night
what touched you most
were the hands of Rodin;

they were not Rodin's actual hands,
rather they were hands made by Rodin,
four hands set on three stands.

three hands of plaster the color of sand,
and one hand beautifully bronzed and tanned.
in a line these hands were set on their stands
these four hands, these hands of Rodin;

at the museum last night
what touched you most
were these four hands of Rodin.

on the left on its stand
a right hand of Rodin,
of plaster the color of sand.

on the right, a left hand,
this too on a stand,
beautifully bronzed and tanned,
this, too, a hand of Rodin.

the left, on the one hand, smaller,
and pointing one finger
touching the air,
the right, on the other hand, taller,
with two fingers pointing,
these, too, touching the air.

and they touched you
these hands of Rodin
their fingers lingering
touching the air,
one left hand, one right hand
each set alone on a stand.

but touching you most
were the other two hands;
two right hands together
set on one stand
set between the stands
of the other two hands,
these two hands of Rodin,
these, too, their fingers, lingering,
touching the air.

four hands on three stands,
all hands of Rodin.

but touching you most
were those two right hands
set on one stand.
two right hands the color of sand
these, too, hands of Rodin,

one hand was my hand
the other hand yours,
they were our hands,
these hands of Rodin.

both hands open, palms facing left
two different right hands,
one yours, one mine
both set on one stand,

your hand inside my hand
my fingers touching
the fingers of your hand.
lingering our fingers and hands,
the touch of these hands of Rodin
becoming the touch of our hands.

and this touched you most:
this touch of our hands
there in the hands of Rodin.

early evening high in the hills

jazz and rain...

I.

in Montessori shadows
early evening high in the hills
jazz and rain.
miracles of biology way back
in the cabin; warm, safe.
new adventures in childhood,
remembering places we'd never been.

II.

on the marina's edge
early evening on the bay
front seat, back seat, wet seat
clear lights of the city
far, far away.

o young fig,
lush rascal
under the leaf
barely exposing
how ripe you are,
tender
tentative
tempting—
plumped bottom
rounded green
and amber,
purple half moon
skin too delicate to peel,
dew beads caress
your neck's curves
slipped from the noose,
your stem salutes me.

o, quivering Calimyrna,
petite Black Mission,
delicious fig
drunk on your own sugars
and my drizzling reductions
you tease the tongue's first press

o. my young fig.

how shall I have you today?

with your salt and tang
before letting loose
your mellifluous perils
like swallows flying
across honey wine skies.

dried by naked sunlight
your shimmering crystalline skin
bathes back to succulence
with a sprinkling of vinaigrette
and mixed greens;

or picked fresh,
and skewered with rosemary,
flames lick you
into sweaty, sweetening softness.
you keep me coming
back for more...

o, my young fig,
how shall I have you today?

On the night of the shooting stars
the sky is clear.

I watch you standing by the window
staring through the open blind
at the brightness of the stars
against the cold dark.

Earlier at dinner
formal and distant
surrounded by crystal and etiquette
and a life we would never live,
I stared at you

through a centerpiece
of red mum and eucalyptus
and beneath the hum of conversations
on work and weather I remembered
that corner of my night
where you first appeared,
the black space where you quickly faded.
I wondered,
are you not a shooting star
seen once and never seen again?

And here you are now
watching for your own shooting star
to cut through this atmosphere
of clouds and fears
forming in this long sad year.
your head turned up
looking past the moon
into chasms
crackling with cold winter air.

In this city tonight
there's no one else like you
no one with such a window
open to the shooting stars
no one whose head turns up
to see what burns tonight
for no one's eyes save yours.

In the morning, the sunlight
streaming through the glass
warms our bodies and our touch
as if the cold of the night itself
had faded with the shooting stars
seen once and never seen again.

In the morning, the sunlight

streaming through the glass

warms our bodies

and our touch

boundaries quiver around the body;
alive, breathing
like valves in the heart,
letting love in, letting love out.
keeping the self whole,
dancing to its rhythms,
its singular discrete code,
its certain consistent pulse,
becoming uniquely more and more
exactly who already is.
being one, protecting the place
for playing with plurals,
with opposites,
the blue blood and red
turning each to the other
in its time, not wearing down,
not losing the boundaries.

giving is different
than giving up.

giving your self is
different than giving up
who you are, or

giving up the ground
you grow from, the sky
where your flight expands
and you move freely—giving
your self is different than
giving up boundaries.

in love there is giving
and no giving up,
no surrender of space,
no break down of boundaries,
no letting blood gush
and flood and flow and empty
reservoirs into mad rivers;
no stiffening either,
no damming the boundaries
and letting pools stagnate, breed fevers,
breed pests.
in love there is giving:
harmony, balance
two separate others ebbing and flowing
filling up, letting out, taking back,
giving everything;
giving up nothing at all.

a new sun kissing the face of dark planets

love upholds the best in us,
keeps the best available
for the giving that is good,
replenishes the best
even as we give and give again;
in the giving love makes best better.
love plays no part in giving up,
love doesn't lose the sacred space,
love keeps it like a hearth creating
waves of heat, creating,
a new sun kissing the dark face of planets,
warming their whole wideness with solar winds—
invisible, intense, inexhaustible.

love doesn't give up
the self,
doesn't give up the particular shine
one has in the world,
doesn't give up the solitary space
where we drink again and again
the lonely waters, where we connect
with the knowing of alone, so we know
about giving and giving up.
giving up surrenders the honest mirror

giving up smears dirty grease on the diamonds
giving up stunts the growth of hardwood,
the nest building, the crackling
of the kitchen fire.
in giving up we lose what we have to give,
lose touch, lose even the winter moments
when the cold brightens us.

giving is different than giving up.
in giving we gain ourselves,
we spread ourselves outward
like the plant from the roots,
the plant giving flowers and seeds,
not giving up roots, not giving up
its own place in the dark soil.

giving without giving up.
giving, illuminated heart,
boundaries moving in,
moving out;
letting love in,
letting love out.

more than a glimmer in my eye
or my rise
when you lean into me,
our unconceived child
appears at odd moments,
along vacant early morning streets
where house by house she shows me
how she places the pumpkins
size by size on the steps,
how she hangs the ornamental corn
on doorways; she reminds me
she is seeking a passageway;
she nudges me, her father,
who will take her to the fair.
she waits
for your answer.

her waiting is the waiting I feel,
like your longing for ocean
and the play of dogs around a garden.
she waits for her entry,
she hovers around the breathing
of our open mouths and the fire
in our spines.
she slept well on the night
I asked you to marry me.

wanting to be here,
she guides my fantasies
when in the moments before sleep,
having only thoughts of you to hold me,
I lead my hands to myself
to lingam and chest and thighs;
and my mind to delicate wanderings
around memories of your body
conjured up from a dim past
when we slept on either side of a chasm
we then couldn't cross.
I explore especially your wrinkles and hair,
the shape of your toes, the blue vein
in your forehead, the thicknesses
that delight her, seeing, as she does,
the endless possibilities in our combining
sweat and genes.

I rest my head on your open thigh
opening my lips to the warm
passageway that she and I will share.
I whisper, I kiss, preparing the way
for pleasures, for the tender opening
and for the difficult strain,
the exhausting stretch
even now you are just beginning.

and my mind to delicate wanderings

around memories of your body

Ti Chiedi

You Wonder

55

Ti chiedi
se spariro,
come un arcobaleno
dopo la pioggia
quando la luce del sole
ascuiga le lacrime
delle nuvole.

You wonder
if I will disappear,
like a rainbow
after the rain
when sunlight
dries the tears
of the clouds.

Ma non sparisco,

invece appaio,

sto sempre apparendo

nel cambio delle stagioni,

nello spazio in cui la luna tira la marea,

nei momenti di chiaroscuro.

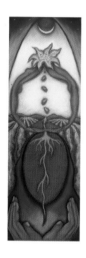

But I do not disappear,

instead I do appear,

I am always appearing

in the change of the seasons,

in the space where the moon pulls the tides,

in the moments of dusk.

Appaio qui,

e tu sempre mi scopri

in questo momento que scorre

e nel prossimo, e prossimo, e prossimo

I appear here,

and you will find me always

in the flow of this moment

and in the next one,

and the next, and the next

...you are so full of wonders

that I will remember you

in my next life.

harmony

Snowflakes

I.

stars sleeping softly
across meandering skies,
still dreaming snow flakes.

II.

snow flakes drift, settle
on boughs of cherry blossom,
awakening white.

III.

morning birds singing
snow flakes disappear, lightly
you rise in my arms.

this rich lush miracle

of nature's lovely balanced labor...

Miracles of the Vine

what astonishes everyone most at the wedding
is that the best is saved for last.

the host, knowing there is nothing left in the cellar,
smiles coyly at his steward's apparent sleight of hand;
and ebullient with this impossible wine,
he savors his guests' delight.
Ah, the bouquet of this miracle of hospitality!

some guests, relishing a quick fix
to turn the dance lighter,
the tempo quicker, the singing more boisterous,
and the coupling less discrete,
barely taste the new wine's whole richness
and lose the longer, more surprising finish.

others, though seeing the stunning ferment
of a supple mind creating,
accelerating the ordinary into the uncommon,
do not appreciate the subtle hints
of pineapple, mango
and soft oak;

they do not notice the magic of this rich, lush miracle,

of nature's lovely balanced labor:
roots drawing water from soil,
vines extending to sunlight,
growing flesh of fruit
sweetness finely turned to spirit.

it happens every season
day by day,
miracles
in ordinary appearances;
in every vine, every taste,
the miracles we savor,
taking so long, becoming so common,
barely seeing them happen at all.

what astonishes me most about you
is your living at the edge of miracle,
creating the best out of a long, late harvest.
making it last

miracles of the vine
complex and full bodied
pour slowly.

what astonishes me most about you

is your living at the edge of miracle...

Love Making

I.

leopard spots, long hair.
no touches like this for months,
cat purrs; so do I

II.

the backs of my thighs
suddenly taut and muscular
exercises of love
with you
I bend back the bow
I release
and touch your targets

III.

orchards of peach and pear
fields of strawberry
blackberries everywhere

IV.

oceans tide one into other
fragrant salts, lips of mussel,
the satisfying pinks of sunlight
near the bay and hills and waves

V.

sometimes you quiver
or shake, or roll
sometimes you moan
and call the names of heaven

VI.

your arms, legs
angel wings,
the whole plane of you
a surf of passion,
your opal eyes,
the air of your lungs
sweet, refreshing

VII.

finally my seeds find fertile soil
I give them now to you
wanting to plant every last one

Buon Natale

tonight I am with baby Jesus.
Joseph, his father, bewildered
in the small shelter where birth has happened;
Joseph, shivering, as the light comes into darkness.

tonight I am with you,
the light of my life,
the fire in the star.
you, gentle mother, sister,
mi amor.

tonight our baby is born
and already I dream of our travels
with him to Egypt, escaping Herod,
and further on to the fragrant soft seas,
to the cottage at the end of the earth,
where together all the children dance.

72

tonight you bring love to the world,
perfect and pure, to the cold
you bring heat. you still my shivering.

tonight I tame the wolves
howling in your heart,
I tend your gardens.
and there in your arms
our baby will be safe.

tonight, loving us
forever after.

Love Song for All

you are so full of wonders
that I will remember you
in my next life

that when I come back again
as an apple tree
I will devote
a whole year's growth to you

you will be apples

from winter sleep
to blossom
to bud
to summer leaves
to ripe fruit falling
on autumnal ground

feeding bird
and beetle
earth
and tree

76

LIST OF PLATES

ABOUT THE ARTIST, JULIE HIGGINS

"My work has a symbolic nature deeply rooted in the places I have lived. I was born in Kansas and received a BFA in painting and sculpture from the University of Kansas; the heartland landscape and its organic forms made strong impressions on me. My time spent in the fertile Skagit Valley in Washington State further influenced my compositions and my current locale on the Mendocino Coast continues to inspire me to illustrate symbolically this sensual environment.

"I work primarily with soft pastels due to their vibrant color and tactile quality. The process is very intuitive, with color, form, imagery, and symbols often leading from one to the next, producing a series of works with ongoing similar themes. Pastels give me the sense of sculpting as I work on paper blending colors with my fingers, molding and giving shape to forms. I love working with the figure, and particularly the female figure, because to me it is the most familiar and interesting in terms of shape, volume, and similarity to the landscape. The act of creating for me is often like a meditation and place to focus allowing for deep feeling and emotion to arise and then translate into image.

"The main themes in my work are based around healing, celebration of love and life, using figures set in a rich landscape with ravens and the luscious fruits that echo the areas' own fertile harvests. Ravens are protector figures, sometimes humorous and other times serious, influenced by the mythology of the indigenous people of the Pacific Northwest.

"My work is a constant process of storytelling and pushing through the mundane of life into the magic, and the imaginary, which connects me to my sense of nature and how I belong or fit in. It is feeling, emotion, and play set in an ever-nurturing landscape with sensual form and lots of color. Joe and I found common themes in our work and so decided to present them together—words and images arising from the heart."

Higgins currently lives on the Mendocino coast of northern California where she continues to express her participation in the feast of life through images as a symbolic language. She hangs several much anticipated shows annually throughout wine country and is honored to be the Artist in

Residence at Sondra Bernstein's restaurant, *the girl and the fig*, in Sonoma, California. Her work has been exhibited in numerous galleries and museums as well as many alternative venues and can be found in private collections nationwide.

ABOUT THE POET, JOE PULICHINO

"Poetry writing has long been my avocation. I was born in Paterson, New Jersey—proudly so because the Silk City is the hometown of William Carlos Williams and Allen Ginsberg, both of whom continue to inspire and influence my writing greatly. From my early teens, I was reading and writing poems and through them discovered a wonderful way of looking at the world and experiencing life. This perspective has since stayed with me. I studied literature at Boston College and Rutgers University, and taught poetry and creative writing at Douglass College. After a few years of teaching, I began a long career in adult learning, ultimately receiving a doctorate in education from Pepperdine University. All the while I've continued writing, reading new poets, participating in the occasional workshop, and bit by bit learning the craft. I felt called to poetry—a mysterious, delightful diversion in the midst of day-to-day life that also happens to explain that life. I enjoy poetry that speaks from and to the heart, stimulates the mind, and ignites the spirit. To the extent my own poems do any of these things, I owe to the many poets—ancestors and contemporaries, celebrated and not—from whom I have learned this timeless art form.

"Recently, I rediscovered many of the poems I had written over the past three decades. Stuffed away in various and unorganized folders, boxes, and drawers, these poems were rarely published, only sometimes read out loud, and most often written and given to a friend or lover just to say what they say. Some were fairly new, some very old. Some were written and then left alone, some later edited and reworked assiduously. As I read through them all, I found that seventeen of the poems, though written at many different times in my life, could be sequenced as a story—a love story that traces the arc of a relationship from beginning to end. Thus, were born the *Love Songs of a Zen Romantic*. Soon after, the idea came to publish these poems in a book along with complementary, illuminating artwork. That path led to Julie and her wonderful collection of brilliant, exuberant pastels. When I first saw them, I knew immediately that her pastels and my poems were a match made in heaven. Now they've taken up together in this little book, *Illuminated Heart*, where they'll live together happily ever after—or so a Zen Romantic would hope."

Dr. Pulichino currently lives in the North Beach neighborhood of San Francisco where he relishes his neighbors' appreciation for art, music, and poetry and enjoys the caffé lifestyle, *la buona cucina*, and fabulous Bay views. He continues to write as the Muse inspires and to work in his beloved field of education. *Illuminated Heart* represents the first publication of his poems in book form.

ACKNOWLEDGEMENTS

Julie Higgins and Joe Pulichino wish to express their gratitude to all those whose support, encouragement, and advice made this book possible, especially Christine Ardito, Paul Deaton, Cynthia Frank, Mara Mauri Jacobsen, Dan Lieuw, Rich Piellisch, Alexander Pulichino, Matthew Pulichino, Anthony Santoro, Carol Simone, Linda Spector, Bill Vesterman, Julie Vetter, and Theresa Whitehill, along with our many family and friends who have always been there for us. Deepest gratitude is extended to Sondra Bernstein, who honors Julie as an artist by exhibiting her artwork year-round at *the girl and the fig*, and has given her full support to this project. We also would like to acknowledge and thank our parents—Boyd and Virginia Higgins, and John and Agnes Pulichino—for teaching us to love, and for all their love and support throughout our lives.

CREDITS

Illuminated Heart: Love Poems of a Zen Romantic was typeset in Janson Text, with P22 Dearest Script for titles and quotes. Text pages were printed and varnished on 157 gsm Lumi Silk Artpaper. The casebound cover with cloth wrap spine was printed on 128 gsm Lumi Silk Artpaper over boards with Saifu cloth wrap spine.

BOOK DESIGN AND PRODUCTION:
THERESA WHITEHILL, COLORED HORSE STUDIOS
UKIAH, CALIFORNIA, *www.coloredhorse.com*

BOOK MANUFACTURING: GLOBAL INTERPRINT
SANTA ROSA, CALIFORNIA

To inquire about purchasing giclée prints
from the pastels of Julie Higgins,
please contact the artist:
(707) 937-4707
Post Office Box 1562
Mendocino, CA 95460
www.artistjuliehiggins.com